Brown Cheese Please

jenny k blake: brown cheese please

© Schibsted-Forlagene AS, Oslo 2003

5. opplag, 2006

design: jenny k blake

trykk og innbinding: AIT Trykk Otta AS

ISBN 10: 82-516-2042-2

ISBN 13: 978-82-516-2042-0

Brown Cheese Please

norway inside out from the outside in

written & illustrated by jenny k blake

SCHIBSTED
FORLAGENE

to my family: heather, kerry
& kim & to jan kenneth

og ett tusen milliarder takk
til turid, arvid, farmor,
og aagård familien fra sandøya
som har lært meg så mye om dette
fine landet, Norge. takk også til
anne-marit, robert og tobias.

norge

This little book, despite
rampant generalizations,
is written with utmost
respect for the norwegian
people, their culture and
the most beautiful land
in which they live,
the kingdom of norway.

vær så god...

observation № 1
NORWAY was once inhabited by ferocious sea-faring vikings!

observation № 2
Vikings didn't actually wear horned helmets, although they were discovered in Denmark in the Bronze Age. the only similar example found in viking times were helmets with bird's heads attached, or in some cases, whole birds!

observation № 3
the cheese slicer, a groundbreaking norwegian invention, wasn't created until 1923. Hence it may be concluded that this image of a pillaging female viking, with a horned helmet and a cheese slicer in hand must have been created by a somewhat naive foreigner. YUP!

brown cheese please

innhold — stuff inside

inhabitants

norwegians, nordmenn og

noen med eksepsjonelt stor nese

jippiii...!

the norwegian male

(may, on occasion, be affectionately
referred to as a "weegie")

: the essence of the generic norwegian male,
slugs and snails and puppy dogs tails comes pretty close.

available in peace activist, environmentalist, friluftsliv*,
handyman, family-man, entrepreneur and shaved-headed,
glasses-wearing, business-suit models.

* friluftsliv model displayed

Cotton shirt: check, chambray or khaki only. (Stripes accepted at Majorstua)

scarf: not too tightly wrapped if you're looking at keeping your weegie longterm.

a really warm, woolly beanie: most weegies will be reluctant to remove these long enough for washing. hence the wet sheep smell occasionally detected.

windproof, watertight gore-tex jacket: either of the 2 leading norwegian brands acceptable.

Prickles: usually acquired on weekend cabin trips. treat with caution.

Y front boxers: no explanation.

loverly beige woollen thermal top.

gore-tex pants: khaki most popular. be aware if in the mountains in autumn you may well sit on a weegie before you see him.

birch handled knife: usually only used when cheese slicer is unavailable.

Woollen thermals: Y fronts also.

especially hairy legs: for extra thermal protection.

Sturdy hiking boots: leather, suede or gore-tex with a good spread of mud stuck in the soles.

Woolly socks: moisture wicking for sweaty weegie feet.

accessory № 1
a sturdy backpack, sitting mat, tur kopp & appropriate equipment for present season or laptop for weekdays.

accessory № 2
a trusty, bird-hunting, bell-wearing, stick-retrieving rover.

the norwegian female

(also referred to under the
generic term "weegie")

: the essence of the norwegian female
is everything <u>but</u> sugar and spice
and all things nice.

also available in peace activist, environmentalist,
friluftsliv and entrepreneur, in addition to
kunstig, miss bogstadveien and husmor special.

* friluftsliv model displayed

Clothing as per norwegian male, Y fronts included. Additional industrial strength chest protection also required for undulating norwegian terrain.

accessory № 1

a bundle of wool and gore-tex, and perhaps a norwegian child in there... somewhere.

accessory № 2

a contented, sturdy, durable infant willing to ride in strange baby backpacks, little carts behind bicycles and in some bizarre contraptions on snow.

accessory № 3

a life support system for accessories 1 & 2, containing various examples of norwegian cuisine as outlined in chapter 6. In addition, clothing and outdoor equipment appropriate for both in and outdoor use for temperatures between −25°c & +25°c recommended.

the norwegian troll

: the essence of the generic norwegian troll; earth, water, fire, air and a good measure of dirty socks.

HABITAT: trolls can mostly be found high up in the mountains, stuffed under tree roots or awaiting your arrival in dark caves or cheap, badly positioned caravan parks.

big nose: to smell out lost hikers, boaters or naive tourists who happen to wander into their realm.

light averting eyes: because all "nasties" try to avoid the sun; they're concerned it will damage their complexion.

hairy: so they can lay down flat and pretend they're a feild of grass to fool oncoming victims.

Walking stick: to navigate through the rugged terrain. Also used to keep occasionally explosive populations of lemmings at bay.

smelly: because as the common myth goes - if it looks bad, it probably smells bad to.

ugly feet: because ugly trolls have ugly feet

available in huldra, skogstroll (skautroll), dravgen, nixie, fossegrimen and jutultroll models among others, regardless, they're all pretty ugly excluding the huldra variety, who resembles a kind of cow woman thingy. * skogstroll model displayed

(under no circumstances to be confused with a nisse, a kind of nice little elfy thing)

what makes norwegians norwegian

flagg, fjells, tax fri

not imperialistic. just a flag on a stick.

front elevation as seen from road

side elevation as seen from

behind the bushes

abroad

norge

the closer you are to nature,
the more alive you feel.
the closer you are to nature,
the more dead you smell.

a chain of self - conscious confusion:

five norwegians each wondering

what the other is thinking

the meat kid syndrome

usually affects norwegian children within 12 hours of returning from a meat, beer and lolly extradition tour across the provocative swedish border. symptoms often develop under the heightened atmosphere amid too many trays of prime swedish rump steaks, danish chickens, beer in blue cans and multiple crumpled paper bags half filled with fluorescent coloured, artificially flavored, sugar coated candy.

may experience outbreaks
of psychotic laughter due
to glucose overdose

Strained, averted
eyes from veiwing
multitude of colourful
delights in oversized
swedish shopping malls

Wobbly knees due to
unfortunate combination
of preservatives E340,
E341, E471 with colouring
E160a, E180a and E163b

large lolly bag clutched
desperately in sweating,
sugar-stained palms

symptoms are further agitated by the presence
of three other glucose-saturated juveniles at various
stages of hallucination, hyperactivity and hysteria
in addition to the solitary adult in the
volatile vehicle chanting "please don't stop us,
please don't stop us..." as the four-wheeled,
trance-consumed party makes its way over the
seemingly endless bridge from the wicked
delights of sweden to the scarey seriousness
shrouded over the norwegian toll gates.

typical specimans of wild,
norwegian, nocturnal wildlife.

everything will be okay.
everything will be okay if
i just do what the
others are doing...

norwegian mentality may
have been derived from the
days spent high, high up in
the mountains

as the little weegies slowly grow
older they begin on the long
pilgrimage south to
experience all the
sinful delights of sun, sea
and cheap sangria.

a fine day it was, the sun was shining,
when i took a walk through norway.

i searched, i searched, i hoped to find,
the key to the cultural doorway.

For the norwegians seem, just like their land,
the ruggedness keeping parts hidden.

Far away and hard to reach,
and entry seems forbidden.

<u>weegies at work</u>

corduroy suits & hiking boots

we're expecting
mr. hansen
from norway
today

they're leading
the market in
many areas of
new technology
and design

yes, the
norwegians
are miles ahead.
slick, sophisticated,
cutting edge

we're expecting him
any minute now...

"hall-ow dare.'"

where you find all the
ambitious trolls:
på vei opp trollstigen

LONDON

OSLO

LONDON

OSLO

business etiquette

paris

sydney

goa

moscow

munich

oslo

a day in the life of a troll

somewhere high up in the norwegian
mountains in a damp, dark cave.

i'll just be sitting here waiting for ya,

just sitting here waiting...

way of the weegies

indoors, outdoors or in a queue

å få fred og ro

here we are,
way out in
the rugged
norwegian
wilderness,

where some
strange, mystic
stone formations
have been
reported,

it's presently unknown
by any historian the
significance of these
amazing structures.
do they hold astrological
relevance?

or perhaps
religious?

experts
worldwide
remain
baffled...

den guddommelige pilgrimsreise

hyttetur, det er moro det!

the norwegian
mountains make
me feel all alone.
without feeling
lonely...

norwegian philosophy № 9

the less people you see on a
hike the more successful it is

ss

trollveggen

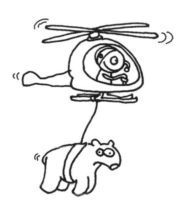

the art of making snow angels
was never quite the same after
"big hair" came into fashion

exposing nordic myth Nº 6: nudity

all the long,
dark, cold winter

the Scandinavians
must walk the
streets hidden

wrapped in multiple layers,
they quietly go about their
everyday lives until —
the first flower of spring appears

then they manically
(but understandably)
tear off the layers

in a desperate search for
the sunshine that has
eluded them all winter

but the sun & light
also brings tourists to
these far off, mystic,
nordic lands

and hence the visitors, some elated,
some disgusted, travel back to their
respective homelands to sit around in
their mild winters wondering about those
wild, free-living, naked scandinavians.

59

ikke ködd med oss—
vi er på bærtur.

something very strange happens
to a norwegian as they pass through
the mystic magnetic forces and head aboard

the   the   the   the
king queen crown crown
              prince princess

the
crown
princess'
father

Lørdag Morgen

beep
02
POST

beep
05
VINMONOPOL
21

beep
07
APOTEK

beep
16
POST
15

beep
22
VINMONOPOL
21

beep
35
APOTEK
35

LUNSJ

sommer

nynorsk

When an outsider comes in

Stupid tourist
thing to do Nº 4:

postpone a trip
out just because
it's raining.

Stupid tourist
thing to do Nº 5:

use the pretty
coloured wax
that came with
your new skiis
on your new
ski boots.

Stupid tourist
thing to do Nº 6:

sneaking past
the beer
curtain
after 8 pm.

Stupid tourist
thing to do Nº 17:

use waterbased face cream
when it's -18°c plus
wind-chill out.

Stupid tourist
thing to do Nº 12:
join a queue of
any kind when you've
got a train to catch
within the next half hour.

the official
"welcome to norway kit"

as required by all new norwegian
residents as a supplement to
the "velkommen til norge" orientation
programme as outlined on the back
of any kvikk lunsj wrapper.

Sitteunderlag
sitting mat. May double as a toboggan in dire circumstances.

Solbærtoddy
blackcurrant drink mix. good. very good. hot or cold.

Kaviar
fish mush in a toothpaste tube (no arguments weegies) it's just plain old fish mush in a toothpaste tube.

Ostehøvel
cheese slicer. it slices cheese, although since it was invented by a norwegian, thor bjørklund, many seem to think it has some strange, mystic powers & the world will fall apart in its absence.

Brun Ost
brown cheese. it's kind of sweet. it's kind of cheesy. it falls apart when the weather gets too hot, it comes in a multitude of varieties. It's pretty much representative of the norwegian people

Joika
canned reindeer.

Norsk flagg
the almighty norwegian flag. If you don't know what to do with it be sure to have a good 2 hours free and any norwegian will be happy to explain when, where & which one's appropriate for the occasion.

Knekkebrød
crispbread. because we all really do like that taste of cardboard.

Ibsen-bok
book by Ibsen. tales from a famous norwegian for those lonely norwegian winter nights.

Friluftslivsutstyr
outdoor equipment. no page is big enough to list all items. NB. all equipment must be current season.

RyggSak
backpack. QUADRUPLE stitched!

Ulltøfler
Wool slippers. totally acceptable in norway. you need not be over 70 or donned in a flowery nightgown with curlers in your blue rinsed hair.

Lommelykt
torch. great for the dark winters & may also act as a self-defence weapon should you be unfortunate enough to encounter a troll.

Ullundertøy
woolen underwear. essential.

Ullsokker
Wild, Woolly Winter Socks for wild Woolly winters.

Engangsgrill
disposable grill. an essential summer accessory that's the death of many a norwegian garbage bin.

Kvikk Lunsj
much debate (presently unresolved) about if they're comparable to another unnamed chocolate bar (most foreigners won't notice the difference - if there is any).

Kaviar

71

the stålis swing

first day in a norwegian office

and i thought he really liked me

one fine day i was lucky enough to be invited to a typical norwegian home for a traditional norwegian meal.

i was so excited as i walked past the hand painted mailbox...

HAR BOR OLE

and up to the red wooden door

my loverly norwegian host greeted me with the traditional "Hei Hei"

i sat down at the wooden table decked with ketchup and toothpicks and wondered what was to come

i sat smiling in anticipation of a traditional norwegian meal.

vær så god, it's called grandiosa!

grandiosa?

75

typical norwegian homes are _very_ interesting

Hei, Hei, velkommen!

just make yourselves at home, back in a second...

wow - look at all these candles! Is this some kind of strange religious ceremony?

Nah... it's just something they call

"Koselig, hyggelig, deilig"

the dark clouds cloaked the forbidding sky,
as i stepped onto the street.

oslo sentral i left behind as i
set out upon my feet.

on this grey day i hoped to find,
that little thing on my way.

that thing that was,
that thing that is,
the epitome of norway.

up the street i hauled myself,
past the beggers tins.

they no longer dance,
they no longer sing,
they just sit there by the bins.

I felt sad, i felt lost,
amid the neon signs.

none of which, i assumed to be,
of the quintessential nordic kinds.

penger
takk

upon the castle i finally came,
with a feeling of stoic pride.

So grand, so nice, so fine it was,
my elation i couldn't hide.

So there i stood, before its facade,
a little waving figure.

but the king wasn't home,
or he didn't see,
— perhaps if i was bigger.

So on my way i dolefully went,
with my head hung low.

if norway's heart wasn't in
the castle, then where was i to go?

i trudged uphill along a street,
of stiff mannequins and fake smiles.

pølser wrappers, plastic bottles and
paper cups, all heaped up in piles.

the further i went,
the slower i walked,
and my mind began to retreat

this quest, this search, this
soul-filled journey almost had me beat.

but then i found a huge iron gate,
with tall lamp posts on either side.

grand and mystic i knew they hid,
something special on the other side.

and there it was, that special treasure,
i'd been hunting all this day.

not in granite, stone or polished bronze,
but in the bushes it lay.

a little bird, a dusty brown, just
sat and didn't flee.

this elfin creature, and all
in nature, is what norway is to me.

vår i oslo

A hairy hat,
a slush drenched mat,
the tram wires
stark on grey.
An oslo street, 
i've missed the beat, 
my scarf's begun to fray.
it's dark, it's cold,
all life is dampened,
the nordic winter 
stands here.
a silence, 
a restraint,
the light so faint,
i hope that spring is near.

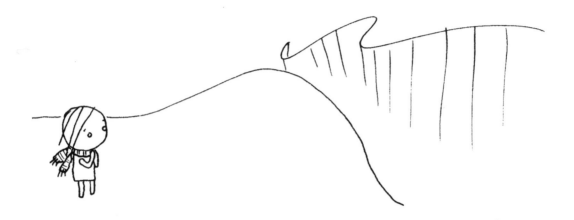

it was a cold, autumn evening. dark, clear, cold.
i took a walk up a still, empty road. the
secretive sky looked down upon me. the
infinite dark expanse looked down upon me.
me, alone on a cold, autumn evening,
alone on a still, but now less empty, road.
suddenly the sky began to sing. the sky
sang blue and green and iridescent turquoise.
it sang and danced and laughed at me there
alone on that road. then it sank. the sky
sank away and i stood alone in the darkness.
there was no applause. the sky just sank away
to darkness and i turned up that still, lonely road
and walked away from that laughing sky. that
dancing, singing, wonderful, but now empty sky.

Oh... you're so lucky,

beautiful brown skin,

gorgeous blue eyes

loverly blonde hair,

i sure wish i was made up of those marvellous scandinavian genes.

genes? It's got nothing to do with genes! it's just solarium, colour contacts and bleach.

this place isn't
nearly as bad
as everyone
makes out

HELL

i once took a train

and then a boat

and then i arrived at a most amazing

place somewhere in the north of norway

and it was amazing

norwegian nutrition

pølser, pikniker, pålegg

modern day burning
at the stake

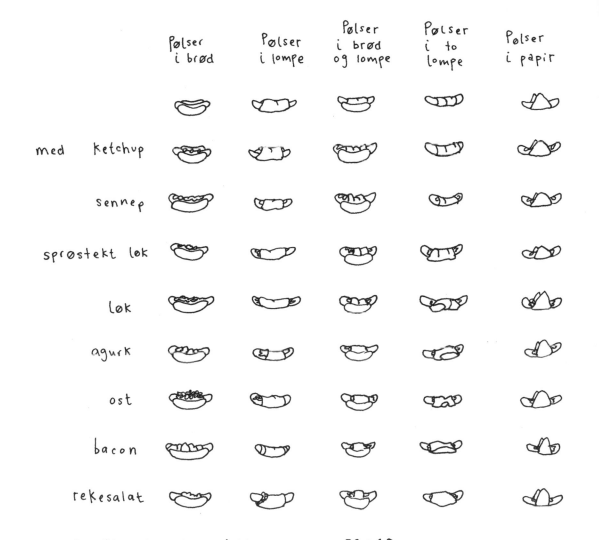

	Pølser i brød	Pølser i lompe	Pølser i brød og lompe	Pølser i to lompe	Pølser i papir
med ketchup					
sennep					
sprøstekt løk					
løk					
agurk					
ost					
bacon					
rekesalat					

Possible pølser permutations approx. 59049
— well in excess of the standard recognized illustrator's comfort zone, even without considering grill or wiener.

frokost

søndag   mandag   tirsdag

onsdag   torsdag   fredag   lørdag

for some strange reason Morten
wasn't feeling quite his usual
self on thursday

pinnekjøtt

rakfisk   tørrfisk

røkt laks   gravlaks

fiskepudding

fiske kake

fiskepinner

fiskeboller

PÅLEGG + BRØD + MELLOMLAGSPAPIR + FOLIE + MATBOKS

= MATPAKKE

Matpakke - (nistepakke) food pack. these
delightful little stashes can be found stuffed
into the pockets, handbags, backpacks and
briefcases of little weegies countrywide.
they are the staple norwegian foodsource
and may be supplemented with waffles
on special occasions.

the art of pålegg

recommended combinations

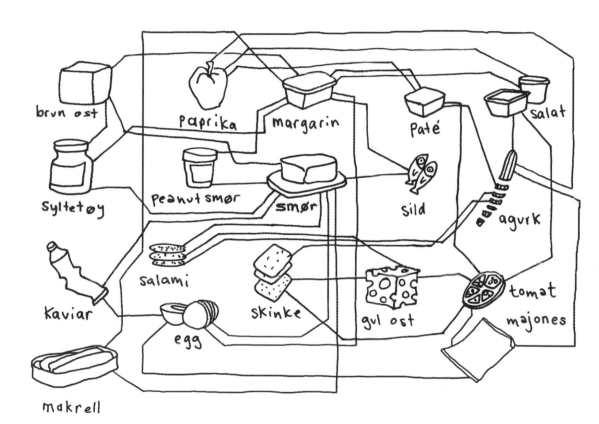

brun ost

paprika

margarin

Paté

salat

syltetøy

Peanut smør

smør

sild

agurk

kaviar

salami

skinke

gul ost

tomat

majones

egg

makrell

NB. no responsibility held for misunderstandings
of chart and consequently the creation of a
potentially lethal pålegg combination.

① construction

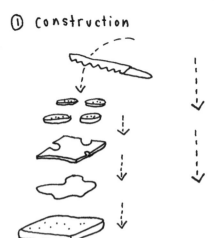

place your selected pålegg carefully onto your selected base. trial and error is, to date, the most reliable bases in which to choose the most appropriate base for your preferred pålegg combination.

DO NOT PLACE ANOTHER PIECE OF BREAD OVER YOUR BASE!

you have now created a typical norwegian "smørbrød". repeat the previous steps if especially hungry.

② preservation

A.
mellomlagspapir

B.

C.
mellomlagspapir

D.

mellomlags papir

take a sheet of custom made "mellomlagspapir" (lay between paper) and carefully stack each smørbrød alternatively with a sheet of paper to protect your pålegg. under no circumstances should a layer of bread be attempted. closed sandwiches are a rare phenomenon in norway and anyone seen eating them will be instantly treated with suspicion.

③ protection

mat folie

lid

matboks

finally wrap your smørbrød stack in greaseproof paper or foil and carefully place it in a matboks, a small, aluminium box, to prevent your precious pålegg stack from being squashed.

close the lid firmly and be on your merry full matboks way.

TA DA - Congratulations,
you have now completed
your first MATPAKKE
and are well on your
way to understanding
the culinary complexities
of the norwegians!

Scene 1: a norwegian attic

silence of the smoked lambs

Arvid thought he'd better call
into Knut's costume hire
before going to buy his
third bottle of wine for
the week

where's my $200
for passing "GO"
man?

olav was in the lead when suddenly
the pleasant game of vinmonopoly
went terribly wrong

a cosy moment with a snoddy:

more commonly known as a solbærtoddy

norwegians don't necessarily drink more
than other nationalities — it's just that
they drink it all at once.

if your brown
cheese just
won't slice,

take a
mellomlagspapir
thin & nice,

lay it down
upon your
cheese,

and slice
a piece as
you please,

or you could
just say
"stuff that!"

and bite
off a
hunk big
& fat

clothing_

the weegie way

how to beat the chain-store phenomenon

Some norwegian
women dress like
they're on the catwalk

Some norwegian
men dress like
they're walking the cat

håvard?

confusion at bodø
barnehage 15:00

the spring lonely hearts club

i've been waiting for the summer collection release for ages...

shh...here comes the first item!

wow!

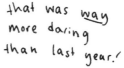

that was way more daring than last year!

gee your bunad sure is pretty. i bet you love wearing it on special occasions...

you bet. it's specially designed...

it's got a super-sharp blade enclosed here, just in case i need to cut off a larger slice of bløtkake

it's got a "too fat tummy" release system here. fully adjustable...

... extra "take with" kransekake storage space here,

perfect for any traditional norwegian celebration

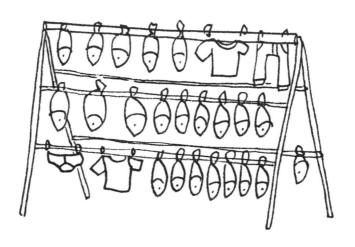

transport

skiis, skates, sleds

spot the norwegian

Korketrekker'n: the bob sled
run from the 1952 oslo olympics
open to the public, not
without consequences, both
fuller emergency rooms
and a sharp decrease
in hairgel sales.

MIDTSTUEN

piggdekk for
underage car
enthusiasts

evolution

it seems nothing escapes the
phenomenon   of   inbreeding
on   small   coastal   islands

the sandøya moped, motorbike & other wheeled apparatus family tree

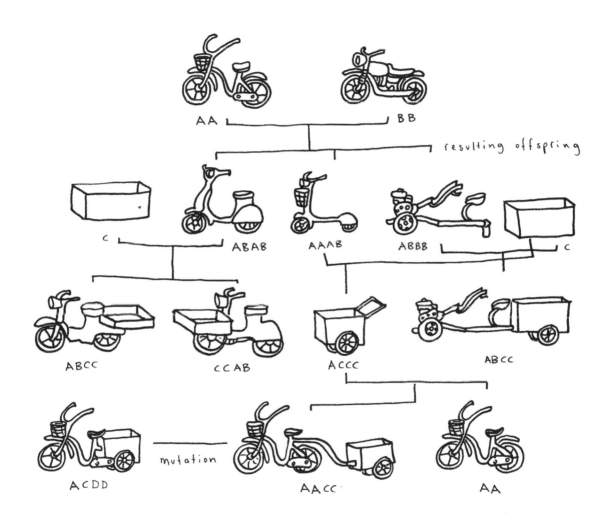

AA   BB

resulting offspring

C   ABAB   AAAB   ABBB   C

ABCC   CCAB   ACCC   ABCC

ACDD   mutation   AACC   AA

131

there exists a common rumour amid
genealogists that many norwegians
have ancestral links with the pack-horse.

<u>traditions</u>

pinse, påske og pepperkakerhus

sankthansaften - pølser

the <u>real</u> scenario of st. Lucia

they were nearing completion when the
pepperkakehus foreman almost lost it

Karl erik was concentrating a
little _too_ hard on playing
his chords right

new year's day –
the annual march of the
gingerbreadmen refugees

pus was delighted someone had
accidently left a chair underneath
Arne's new advent calendar

bibliography

so there it is, all that ive heard & ive seen,
from svalbard to lindesnes & all in between.
whilst talking with grannys out on the street,
or fiddlers from sandane you just happen to meet.
from a farmer in troms who was
loading his silo; to a soggy
wet mitten seen one spring in geilo.
warm, summer nights, enchanting observations;
dark, winter days, woolly contemplations.
it's an intriguing place, this land of fjords;
forests & mountains & weathered boat boards.
of viking graves, sailors & sami reindeer;
& nice little nisses with tempers to fear.

a place of legend with huldras that tease;
the kingdom of norway...
the land of brown cheese.

jkb